CIVIC VALUES

RESPECTING OPPOSING VIEWPOINTS

JEANNE MARIE FORD

Cavendish Square

New York

Published in 2018 by Cavendish Square Publishing, LLC
243 5th Avenue, Suite 136, New York, NY 10016

Website: cavendishsq.com

This publication represents the opinions and views of the author based on his or her personal experience, knowledge, and research. The information in this book serves as a general guide only. The author and publisher have used their best efforts in preparing this book and disclaim liability rising directly or indirectly from the use and application of this book.

All websites were available and accurate when this book was sent to press.

Library of Congress Cataloging-in-Publication Data

Names: Ford, Jeanne Marie.
Title: Respecting opposing viewpoints / Jeanne Marie Ford.
Description: New York : Cavendish Square, 2018. | Series: Civic values | Includes index.
Identifiers: ISBN 9781502629364 (pbk.) | ISBN 9781502629388 (library bound)
| ISBN 9781502629371 (6 pack) | ISBN 9781502629395 (ebook)
Subjects: LCSH: Respect for persons--Juvenile literature. | Respect--
Juvenile literature. | Conduct of life--Juvenile literature.
Classification: LCC BJ1533.R42 F65 2018 | DDC 179.9--dc23

Editorial Director: David McNamara
Editor: Kristen Susienka
Copy Editor: Rebecca Rohan
Associate Art Director: Amy Greenan
Designer: Alan Sliwinski
Production Coordinator: Karol Szymczuk
Photo Research: J8 Media

Printed in the United States of America

CONTENTS

Protagoras of Abdera (*standing*) was a Greek philosopher known as the "father of debate."

CHAPTER ONE

WHAT ABOUT RESPECTING OPPOSING VIEWPOINTS?

Americans come from many different cultures. They have many beliefs. They also share common values. Good citizens are brave, responsible, and honest. They treasure the rights of freedom and equality for all. Those rights cannot exist without respect for others' differences.

What Is Respect?

The word "respect" comes from a Latin word that means "to look again." Respect is about how we view someone or something. True respect is demonstrated through both thoughts and actions. If you offer polite words without meaning them, you are not really paying respect.

Respect comes in several forms. In the United States, children are taught to respect their elders,

Americans are taught to respect the US flag. This soldier is showing respect by saluting the flag.

rules, traditions, and the US flag. Above all, they must respect themselves and practice the golden rule: treat others as they wish to be treated.

"There are two sides to every question."
—Protagoras of Abdera

Agreeing or Not

A **democracy** is a form of government by the people. Citizens elect leaders and must accept the results, no matter who they vote for. Agreeing to disagree is an important part of democracy.

Incivility comes from a Latin word that means "not of a citizen." It is defined as rudeness or lack of

Rudeness is a form of disrespect.

respect. Respect does not have to mean agreement. It does mean listening and trying to understand one another. If citizens cannot disagree civilly, democracy begins to fall apart. Bullying, hatred, and violence can all result from lack of respect for others.

Opposing Viewpoints

Today, many high schools and colleges have **debate** teams. Each team defends one side of an issue.

Seventy percent of Americans believe that incivility in politics is a major problem.

Debaters learn how to support any argument, even if they don't agree with it. The ability to look at an issue from different viewpoints is a valuable life skill.

Sometimes the difference between facts and opinions is easy to see. Multiplication facts are clearly

PROTAGORAS OF ABDERA

Protagoras was an ancient Greek **philosopher**. He is known as the "father of debate." Debate is the art of discussing different viewpoints. Protagoras taught his students how to make effective arguments. Arguing did not mean fighting but rather attempting to persuade. The people of Athens eventually decided that certain topics, such as religion, should not be debated. They burned Protagoras's writings and forced him to leave the city forever.

true. Your favorite ice cream flavor is obviously a matter of opinion.

Other questions are more difficult. Religious beliefs that are factual to some are rejected by others. When people have strong beliefs, they may think of them as fact. They may have trouble understanding how anyone can hold a different viewpoint.

The Puritans (*right*) and Native Americans (*left*) celebrated the first Thanksgiving at Plymouth, Massachusetts.

CHAPTER TWO

HISTORY OF RESPECTING OTHERS IN SOCIETY

Englisth settlers called Puritans came to the New World in the 1600s to practice their faith freely. Freedom of religion is an important American value. However, Americans have not always been **tolerant** of people of other faiths. For example, the settlers soon tried to force Native Americans to abandon their beliefs and become Christian.

A Civil Society

One Puritan named Roger Williams was forced to leave the Massachusetts colony because many people disagreed with his views. In 1636, he founded Rhode Island. There he started a civil society that welcomed colonists of all faiths. He thought it was

Roger Williams founded the colony, and the eventual state, of Rhode Island.

Respecting Opposing Viewpoints

important to allow people to express their true beliefs. However, he was not interested in listening to views that differed from his own. Williams was tolerant but not

"We must learn to live together as brothers or perish together as fools." —Martin Luther King Jr.

always respectful of others' opinions.

Philosophers disagreed with Williams about how to make society more civil. Men like Thomas Hobbes felt that people should keep quiet about their disagreements. On the other hand, philosopher John Locke believed that citizens needed to find common beliefs. Only then could they discuss their differences.

Not Respecting Others

As the United States grew more **diverse**, Catholics, Jews, and Muslims faced **discrimination**. Immigrants

These Italian immigrants pose at their food stall in 1908. Many immigrants experienced discrimination when they first arrived in the United States.

from many countries were often treated with disrespect. So were women and people who were not white.

Civility Today

In today's society, it is almost impossible to ignore our differences. Television brings a wide range of views into almost every home. The loudest voices are usually the ones that get the most attention.

Researchers say there are several reasons for the decrease in civility today. The faster

Many studies have found that modern society is less civil than it has ever been.

pace of life causes people to have less patience. Social media encourages rudeness. Parents and

THE MUSEUM OF TOLERANCE

The Museum of Tolerance opened in Los Angeles, California, in 1993. Its mission is to get people to open their minds and hearts to all people. The exhibits teach that peace depends on everyday acts of kindness. When visitors leave, they are encouraged to go out into the world and make a difference.

Social media can make people more selfish.

schools focus less on teaching manners than they once did. Finally, modern society encourages individuals to focus on themselves. When people are self-centered, they are less likely to try seeing things from other viewpoints.

It is important to remember and practice respect when you can. Respect helps make you a more likeable and respected person in return.

CHRONOLOGY

480–411 BCE Protagoras of Abdera lives and teaches in Greece.

1621 CE The First Thanksgiving is celebrated in Plymouth, Massachusetts.

1636 CE Roger Williams founds the state of Rhode Island.

1588–1679 CE Philosopher Thomas Hobbes lives.

1632–1704 CE Philosopher John Locke lives.

1787 CE The first United States political party forms.

1789 CE The United States Constitution is adopted.

1861–1865 CE The United States Civil War is fought.

1993 CE The Museum of Tolerance opens.

The Founding Fathers met in 1787 at the Constitutional Convention to sign the Constitution.

CHAPTER THREE

RESPECT FOR OPPOSING VIEWS AND THE CONSTITUTION

I n the summer of 1787, a group of men we now call the Founding Fathers met to write the United States Constitution. They had many fierce debates about issues such as slavery and voting rights. They resolved their disagreements through compromise. Only three men refused to sign the finished document.

The First Amendment

The First **Amendment** to the Constitution gives Americans several important rights. It guarantees freedom of speech, religion, and the press. However, there are limits to these rights. For example, words cannot be used to cause physical harm to another person. Lying under oath in court is against the law.

Peaceful assembly is a First Amendment right.

> "I do not agree with what you have to say, but I'll defend to the death your right to say it."
> —Evelyn Beatrice Hall

These First Amendment freedoms also give us great responsibility. Over three hundred million people live in the United States. In order to exist together peacefully, we have to express our opinions with respect. We must also listen with respect to others, even when we don't agree with them.

Political Parties and the Legal System

Today's two major American political parties are the Republicans (elephant) and Democrats (donkey).

The Constitution makes no mention of political parties. However, they have been an important part of the US government since the

HATE SPEECH

Words that are meant to hurt people are known as hate speech. Hate speech usually attacks people of a certain religious group, race, or gender. In many cases, it is protected by the First Amendment. However, if it causes violence, it can be a crime. Some people believe that all speech should be free and legal. Others believe that there should be more restrictions on what people are allowed to say. While it is important to respect others' beliefs, hate speech is a form of intolerance. It never deserves respect.

1800 presidential election. Candidates for office usually come from two major parties: the Democratic and Republican parties. The names and beliefs of these parties have changed over time. Individual politicians have their own views. However, their party usually shapes their beliefs on the main issues.

Researchers have found that rudeness is almost always contagious.

The Constitution also set up the government's legal system. Like political parties, cases in the court system have two sides. The law guarantees each side an attorney and equal time to argue its case. In the end, a judge or jury decides which side wins.

Court cases are decided by judges or juries.

These karate students
show each other
respect by bowing.

CHAPTER FOUR

CIVILITY IN SOCIETY TODAY

I n 1865, the Civil War had been raging for almost four years. Hundreds of thousands of young soldiers had died. After his reelection in 1864, President Abraham Lincoln tried to heal a divided country. He urged citizens to look at even their enemies "with malice toward none, with charity toward all." In April 1865, Lincoln was killed by someone who disagreed bitterly with his views.

Abraham Lincoln was killed shortly after his second inaugural address (pictured here) in 1865.

How to Respect Opinions

Differences of opinion can lead to great stress. They can end friendships. They can cause divorce. Of course, it is impossible to surround yourself with people who agree with you all the time. Therefore, it is important to develop skills for peaceful disagreement.

One of the best ways to respect someone's opinion is to listen. People tend to seek out information that confirms what they already believe. They are often reluctant to try to understand views that differ from theirs.

PERSUASION

When we try to persuade others, sometimes we may not fairly describe the other side of the argument. We might leave out important information. We might try to twist the opposing viewpoint to make it sound less appealing. **Propaganda** is a form of persuasion that is used to promote a cause. It often exaggerates or misleads others on purpose.

"Just as war is freedom's cost, disagreement is freedom's privilege." —President Bill Clinton

Sometimes we misread others' intentions. We may forget to look for views that we have in common. We may resist apologizing. These behaviors all lead to incivility. It is important to consider others' opinions and respectfully disagree if necessary.

DISAGREEMENT

Disagreement is not always a bad thing. Having different beliefs and ideas leads to greater creativity. It leads to compromise and cooperation. Diversity is one of the greatest strengths of the United States.

GLOSSARY

amendment A change to a document, like the Constitution.

debate A discussion about differing opinions.

democracy Government by the people.

discrimination Unfair treatment based on people's differences.

diverse Having many differences.

incivility Rude or offensive behavior.

philosopher A person who studies many different points of view on many subjects.

propaganda Information used to influence people and promote a cause.

tolerant Willing to put up with something.

FIND OUT MORE

Books

Boritzer, Etan. *What Is Respect?* Los Angeles: Veronica Lane Books, 2016.

Thomas, Pat, and Lesley Harker. *Everyone Matters: A First Look at Respect for Others*. Hauppauge, NY: Barron's Educational Series, 2010.

Website

Respect

http://talkingtreebooks.com/definition/what-is-respect.html

Video

How to Magically Connect with Anyone

https://www.youtube.com/watch?v=D4cV8yfgNyI

This TED talk discusses the value of perspective in life and magic.

INDEX

Page numbers in **boldface** are illustrations. Entries in **boldface** are glossary terms.

ABOUT THE AUTHOR

Jeanne Marie Ford is an Emmy-winning television scriptwriter and holds an MFA in writing for children from Vermont College. She has written numerous children's books on a variety of subjects, including government and United States history. She also teaches college English. She lives in Maryland with her husband and two children.